Welcome to the heart of war.
The time: The London Blitz of the early 1940s
MORE HOST
... AND
wooooARRRRRRRwooooooARRRR
rumble-ruuuumble kah-boom
The place: The War Office's top-secret map room under the city of London, where the Royal Air Force (RAF) tracks the movements of planes by radio and takes steps to spare Londoners from German bombs
The man: British Prime Minister Winston Churchill
CAN WE SEND A SQUADRON TO MEET THEM BEFORE THEY GET HERE?
I'M NOT SURE IF IT'LL HAVE ENOUGH TIME, SIR.
HMMM. IS THE ENEMY TOO FAR AWAY FOR OUR GROUND WEAPONS?
YES, IT WOULD APPEAR THEY ARE ... ORDINARILY SPEAKING.

YES, *ORDINARILY.*
WITH PLEASURE!
BUT NOW IS THE MOMENT WE HAVE WAITED FOR – WHEN WE CAN UNLEASH THE EXTRAORDINARY.
YES, IT IS FINALLY TIME TO ROLL OUT OUR NEW **SECRET WEAPON!**
Victory of the Daleks
Written by Peter Gutiérrez
Based on the television script "Victory of the Daleks" by Mark Gatiss

Chapter 1: "Prove It, Doctor"

A few minutes later, in a humble storage room nearby.
The **TARDIS** appears.
Capable of travelling anywhere and 'anywhen', it is the preferred means of transport of …
the Time Lord known only as the Doctor, and his companion, Amy Pond.
The Doctor makes his introductions.
IT'S SO AMAZING TO MEET YOU!
I'M SURE IT IS!
IN ANY CASE, I'M CHARMED AS WELL, MY DEAR.
ALL RIGHT – AT EASE, SOLDIERS!
REALLY, WINSTON? IF YOU'RE *THAT* HAPPY TO SEE US, AREN'T YOU GOING TO HAVE THEM PUT DOWN THEIR WEAPONS?

FORGIVE ME. YOU'VE CHANGED YOUR FACE SINCE I SAW YOU LAST, AND YOU'VE ARRIVED A MONTH LATE. WARTIME TEACHES ONE TO BE CAUTIOUS.
A MONTH LATE? REALLY SORRY. TYPE FORTY TARDIS. YOU KNOW. JUST BREAKING HER IN.
NO MATTER. YOUR TIMING IS GOOD DESPITE YOUR TARDINESS. I JUST GOT WORD THAT MORE GERMAN PLANES ARE ON THEIR WAY.
IN WHICH CASE, AREN'T WE GOING IN THE WRONG DIRECTION – NAMELY, *UP*?
WE STAND AT A CROSSROADS, DOCTOR. QUITE ALONE, AND WITH OUR BACKS TO THE WALL. INVASION IS EXPECTED DAILY.
THAT IS WHY I WILL GRASP WITH BOTH HANDS ANYTHING THAT WILL GIVE US AN ADVANTAGE OVER THE MENACE THAT THREATENS US.
SUCH AS?
SUCH AS WHAT I'M ABOUT TO SHOW YOU. UP HERE ON THE ROOF YOU'LL BE ABLE TO SEE THEM IN ACTION ...

THEM?
THE GENTLEMAN WATCHING THE SKIES IS PROFESSOR EDWIN BRACEWELL, HEAD OF OUR IRONSIDES PROJECT.
HELLO! HOW DO YOU DO?
READY, BRACEWELL?
ON MY ORDER, THEN - READY ... !

FIRE!
puh-KOW!
SOOOOZH!
WHAT WAS *THAT?*
WHATEVER IT WAS, IT CERTAINLY WASN'T HUMAN TECHNOLOGY.
SHOW ME! SHOW ME WHAT THAT WAS!
VERY WELL.
AD-VANCE!!
I COULD BE WRONG, BUT THAT SOUNDED LIKE ...

A DALEK!!
SO WHAT DO YOU THINK? QUITE SOMETHING, EH?
QUITE FRANKLY, I'M WONDERING WHAT IT'S DOING HERE.
I AM YOUR SOLDIER.
WHAT?
I ... AM ... YOUR ... *SOLDIER.*
MY 'SOLDIER'? MORE LIKE MY SWORN ENEMY!
YOUR IDENTITY IS UNKNOWN.
LET'S STOP THIS NONSENSE, SHALL WE? YOU KNOW WHO I AM.

PERHAPS I CAN CLARIFY THINGS HERE. THIS IS ONE OF MY IRONSIDES.
YOUR *WHAT?*
YOU WILL HELP THE ALLIED CAUSE IN ANY WAY THAT YOU CAN?
YES.
UNTIL OUR ENEMY HAS BEEN UTTERLY SMASHED?
YES.
AND WHAT IS YOUR ULTIMATE AIM?
TO WIN THE WAR!
OH, I'M SURE – BUT WHICH WAR? *WHOSE* WAR?
PROVE IT, DOCTOR? ON THE CONTRARY, COME WITH ME BACK TO MY OFFICE AND I'LL BE GLAD TO SHOW YOU ...
WINSTON, THEY ARE CALLED 'DALEKS'. GIVE ME A MOMENT. I WILL THINK OF HOW TO PROVE TO YOU THAT THEY ARE MY ENEMY AND *YOURS*.

BLUEPRINTS, FIELD TESTS AND PHOTOGRAPHS. ARE YOU SATISFIED NOW, DOCTOR? CLEARLY BRACEWELL INVENTED THE IRONSIDES!
INVENTED THEM? OH, NO, NO!
I'M TELLING YOU, BRACEWELL APPROACHED ONE OF OUR BIGWIGS A FEW MONTHS AGO. FELLOW'S A GENIUS.
I DON'T DOUBT HE'S A GENIUS – A GENIUS AT FOOLING YOU, IF NOTHING ELSE. BESIDES, HE *COULDN'T* HAVE INVENTED THEM! THEY'RE ALIEN.
ALIEN? YOU MEAN FROM A FOREIGN POWER?
NO, I MEAN 'ALIEN' AS IN ALIEN WORLD. AS IN ... NOT OF THIS EARTH.
And so the Doctor provides a brief history of the Daleks, explaining that their machine-like appearance is only a kind of a shell. They are, in fact, living beings who always have conquest in mind.
Beings who will not hesitate to destroy completely any who stand in their way.

THE DALEKS HAVE NO MERCY, NO PITY. THEY ARE MY OLDEST AND DEADLIEST FOE ...
IN SHORT, DESPITE THE OBEDIENCE THEY'RE SHOWING YOU ... THEY ARE **COMPLETELY HOSTILE**!
YOU CANNOT TRUST THEM!
YES, DOCTOR, BUT HOSTILE *TO WHOM*?
I SAY THEY'LL HELP WIN THIS WAR. NOW, IF YOU'LL EXCUSE ME, I NEED TO MOVE ALONG AND DO JUST THAT ...
EXCUSE YOU? IF YOU'RE NOT GOING TO LISTEN TO WHAT I HAVE TO SAY, WHY DID YOU CALL ME?
WHEN I RANG YOU, I MUST ADMIT I HAD DOUBTS. THE IRONSIDES SEEMED TOO GOOD TO BE TRUE.
THEY *ARE*!
YOU NEED TO DESTROY THEM! EXTERMINATE THEM!
WHO'S HOSTILE NOW?
THE GERMANS ARE WORKING ON EVER MORE POWERFUL WEAPONS. WHY CAN'T WE HAVE OUR IRONSIDES? IMAGINE WHAT I COULD DO WITH A HUNDRED! A THOUSAND!
I AM IMAGINING. THAT'S THE PROBLEM.

THE PROBLEM IS THAT WE EXPECT HIM TO LISTEN TO US ABOUT THE DALEKS WHEN WE HAVEN'T GIVEN HIM ANY PROOF.
WHAT DID YOU HAVE IN MIND?
WELL, PERHAPS WE SHOULD GO STRAIGHT TO THE HORSE'S MOUTH ...
AMY, WHAT ARE YOU ...?
PARDON ME, BUT MY FRIEND KNOWS YOU TO BE DANGEROUS, AND I HAPPEN TO AGREE WITH HIM.
I AM YOUR SOLDIER.
YEAH. GOT THAT BIT. BUT WHAT IS YOUR GAME?
I DO NOT UNDERSTAND. PLEASE EXCUSE ME. I HAVE DUTIES TO PERFORM.
I'LL THANK YOU AND MISS POND TO LET US CARRY ON WITHOUT INTERFERENCE.
WINSTON, PLEASE!
MAY I REMIND YOU, DOCTOR, THAT DAY AFTER DAY, THIS GREAT CITY IS BEING POUNDED AS IF BY AN IRON FIST.
WAIT UNTIL THE DALEKS GET STARTED.
PICTURE THE ENTIRE EARTH IN FLAMES!
MUCH OF THE EARTH IS ALREADY IN FLAMES, DOCTOR. YOU'RE ASKING ME TO MAKE AN ENEMY OF AN ALLY WHEN THE REAL ENEMY ATTACKS US NIGHT AND DAY. THESE MACHINES ARE OUR ONLY HOPE!
Disappointed, the Doctor again seeks out his companion.
WE'RE DOOMED, I TELL YOU ...

Chapter 2: "I Am The Doctor!"

ALL RIGHT, SOLDIER –
DEFEND YOURSELF!!
CLANG!!!
MAKE HIM STOP, PRIME MINISTER! MAKE HIM PUT DOWN THAT WRENCH!
DOCTOR, PLEASE!
COME ON! FIGHT BACK! YOU KNOW YOU WANT TO! WHAT ARE YOU WAITING FOR?
SO ... YOU DO NOT DESIRE TEA?
TEA AGAIN?! LISTEN, YOU HATE ME. YOU WANT TO KILL ME. WELL, GO ON, THEN. THAT IS WHAT I DESIRE – FOR YOU TO SHOW YOUR TRUE COLOURS!
KILL ME!
How did things reach such a boiling point?
To answer that, we'll have to do a bit of time-travelling ourselves – back to that distant period known as ...

two minutes ago.
WOULD YOU CARE FOR SOME TEA?
THAT WOULD BE VERY NICE, THANK YOU.
SORRY TO INTERRUPT, PROFESSOR, BUT COULD YOU EXPLAIN HOW YOU CAME UP WITH THE IDEA FOR THE IRONSIDES?
IDEAS JUST SEEM TO BURST FROM MY HEAD! I DON'T KNOW WHERE MOST OF THEM COME FROM.
HERE, LET ME SHOW YOU SOME OF THEM ...
YOUR TEA ...
THANK YOU.
ARE YOU QUITE SURE THESE IDEAS ARE YOURS, PROFESSOR, NOT *THEIRS*?
!
WE'VE HAD ENOUGH OF THAT, DOCTOR. NOW YOU'RE BEING INSULTING, IF NOT OFFENSIVE.
INSULTING? OFFENSIVE ...?

And so that is how we arrived at … NOW.

PLEASE STOP STRIKING ME. I AM YOUR SOLDIER.
NO!
YOU …
CLANG!
ARE …
MY …
CLUNG!
CLANG!
ENEMY!
AND I AM YOURS! I'VE DEFEATED YOU TIME AND TIME AGAIN!
I AM THE DOCTOR! AND YOU ARE THE DALEKS!!
CORRECT.
REVIEW TESTIMONY.
TESTIMONY? WHAT ARE YOU TALKING ABOUT?
I AM THE DOCTOR! AND YOU ARE THE DALEKS!
TRANSMITTING TESTIMONY NOW.
TRANSMIT WHAT? AND …

WHERE?
The far side of the moon – often called its dark side …
RECEIVING TESTIMONY NOW.
beep beep beep beeeeeeeeeep!
I AM THE DOCTOR! AND YOU ARE THE DALEKS!
PROGENITOR ACTIVATED. TESTIMONY ACCEPTED! TESTIMONY ACCEPTED!

GET BACK! ALL OF YOU!
MARINES! MARINES! GET IN HERE!
But no sooner do the Marines arrive ...
ZZZZZ-CRAAACK!
NO!
WHAT ARE YOU DOING?! YOU ARE MY IRONSIDES!
WE ARE THE DALEKS!
BUT I CREATED YOU!
NO!
WE CREATED YOU!
GASP!
VICTORY! VICTORY! VICTORY!!
And with that, the Daleks teleport to their ship ...

WHAT JUST HAPPENED, DOCTOR?
I WANTED TO KNOW WHAT THEY WANTED, WHAT THEIR PLAN WAS.
I WAS THEIR PLAN!
Meanwhile, on the Daleks' ship, those plans continue to unfold.
BEGINNING PHASE TWO. THE PROGENITOR IS ACTIVATED!
YES, IT BEGINS!
WE NEED ONLY WAIT NOW . . .
"TESTIMONY ACCEPTED" - THAT'S WHAT THEY SAID. MY TESTIMONY - WHICH MEANS I'VE HELPED THEM SOMEHOW.
DON'T BEAT YOURSELF UP. YOU WERE RIGHT ABOUT THEM. THE QUESTION IS, WHAT DO WE DO NOW? CHASE AFTER THEM?
YES AND NO. I CHASE AFTER THEM. BUT IT'S DANGEROUS, SO PLEASE WAIT HERE.
AND IT'S SAFE DOWN HERE? IN THE MIDDLE OF THE LONDON BLITZ?!?
AS SAFE AS IT GETS AROUND ME.
AND SOMETHING TELLS ME THAT IT'S GOING TO GET A LOT LESS SAFE FROM NOW ON!

Chapter 3: "TARDIS Bang-Bang, Daleks Boom!"

HEY! PUT THAT LIGHT OUT!
WHAT FOOL WOULD DISREGARD THE BLACKOUT LIKE THAT? DOESN'T EVERYONE KNOW THAT THE SKIES ARE DANGEROUS?
SIR. THERE'S AN UNIDENTIFIED OBJECT IN THE SKY. WE CAN'T ACCURATELY FIX ITS POSITION, THOUGH. IT'S TOO FAR UP.
HMMM, MUST BE OUR ALIEN FRIENDS.
WHAT DO YOU THINK, MISS POND? THE DOCTOR'S IN TROUBLE AND NOW WE KNOW WHERE HE IS.
YES, BECAUSE HE'S ON THAT SHIP. RIGHT THERE TO SEE WHAT EVIL SCHEMES THE DALEKS ARE HATCHING NEXT.

THE FINAL PHASE IS STARTING. CHANNEL ALL POWER TO THE PROGENITOR.
WAIT – WHO HAS BOARDED OUR SHIP?
IT IS THE DOCTOR! EXTERMINATE!
WHAT? NOT OFFERING ME ANY TEA NOW?
EX-TER-MI-NATE!
EX-TER-MI-NATE!
WAIT, I WOULDN'T IF I WERE YOU! THIS IS THE TARDIS SELF-DESTRUCT CONTROL. AND YOU KNOW WHAT THAT MEANS. MY SHIP GOES, YOU ALL GO WITH IT.
YOU WOULD NOT USE SUCH A DEVICE.
TRY ME.
As one of the Daleks begins to move forward …
AH, AH, AH – HOLD IT RIGHT THERE! ONE MOVE AND I'LL DESTROY US ALL.
TARDIS BANG-BANG, DALEKS **BOOM**!
AH, NOW THAT'S A GOOD BOY.

THIS SHIP'S PRETTY BEATEN UP, I'D SAY. LIKE YOU.
AS A MATTER OF FACT, WHEN WE LAST MET, YOU WERE AT THE END OF YOUR ROPE. FINISHED.
ONE SHIP SURVIVED.
WE PICKED UP A TRACE. ONE OF THE PROGENITOR DEVICES.
'PROGENITOR'? WHAT'S THAT EXACTLY?
IT IS OUR PAST.
AND OUR FUTURE.
IT CONTAINS PURE DALEK DNA.
THOUSANDS WERE CREATED ... ALL WERE LOST.
SAVE ONE.
OKAY, BUT THERE'S ONE THING I DON'T GET. IF YOU'VE GOT THE PROGENITOR, WHY BUILD BRACEWELL?

IT WAS ... NECESSARY.
BUT WHY ...?
OH, I GET IT! THE PROGENITOR WOULDN'T *RECOGNISE* YOU, WOULD IT? IT SAW YOU AS IMPURE – YOUR DNA UNRECOGNISABLE AS DALEK!
A SOLUTION WAS DEVISED.
YES: ME. THE WHOLE 'TESTIMONY' BUSINESS. IT WAS A TRAP FROM THE START ...
YOU KNEW THAT THE PROGENITOR WOULD RECOGNISE ME, THE DALEKS' GREATEST ENEMY! AND IT WOULD ACCEPT MY WORD.
LEAVE NOW, DOCTOR, OR THE CITY DIES IN FLAMES.
ARE YOU KIDDING? THIS SHIP IS A WRECK – YOU DON'T HAVE THE POWER TO DESTROY LONDON.
YOU ARE CORRECT.
BUT WE CAN WATCH AS THE HUMANS DESTROY THEMSELVES.

WHIIIRRRRRRR
crackle
-crackle
ZZZZ
HHHHHHHHHH!
WHAT THE ...?
NO!
The air raid warden's fear is understandable. London has just announced itself as a target ...

THE GENERATORS WON'T SWITCH OFF! THE LIGHTS ARE ON EVERYWHERE, PRIME MINISTER!
CARELESS TALK COSTS LIVES
HAS TO BE THEM. HAS TO BE THE DALEKS.
THE GERMANS CAN SEE EVERY INCH OF THE CITY – AND THEY'LL DESTROY IT IF WE DON'T DO SOMETHING.
GERMAN BOMBERS SIGHTED OVER THE CHANNEL, SIR.
THE ETA IS 10 MINUTES.
WE CAN'T JUST SIT HERE!
WHAT DO YOU SUGGEST WE DO INSTEAD, MISS POND?
WE'VE GOT TO TAKE THE FIGHT TO THE DALEKS!
HOW? NONE OF OUR WEAPONS ARE A MATCH FOR THEIRS.
WAIT, WAIT, WAIT – **HA!**
IT'S STARING US IN THE FACE! A GIFT!
A GIFT FROM THE DALEKS!!

TURN THOSE LONDON LIGHTS OFF NOW OR I SWEAR I WILL USE THE TARDIS SELF-DESTRUCT!
STALEMATE, DOCTOR. LEAVE US AND RETURN TO EARTH.
OH, THAT'S IT? THAT'S YOUR GREAT VICTORY? YOU LEAVE?
EXTINCTION IS NOT AN OPTION. WE SHALL RETURN TO OUR OWN TIME AND BEGIN AGAIN.
NO, NO, NO! I WON'T LET YOU GET AWAY THIS TIME! I WON'T!
Suddenly, the Daleks back away from the chamber they'd been guarding.
hummmmmmmmmmmmmmmmmm
WE HAVE SUCCEEDED.
DNA RECONSTRUCTION IS COMPLETE!

OBSERVE DOCTOR: A NEW MODEL FOR THE DALEKS AS LIVING BEINGS.
A NEW KIND OF DALEK, THE LIKES OF WHICH THE UNIVERSE HAS NEVER SEEN.
THE BEGINNING OF A NEW GOLDEN AGE!
The Doctor can barely control the terrible emotions he feels as he sees one 'new' Dalek after another take its place next to the others.
YES, THE PROGENITOR HAS TRULY FULFILLED OUR DESTINY!

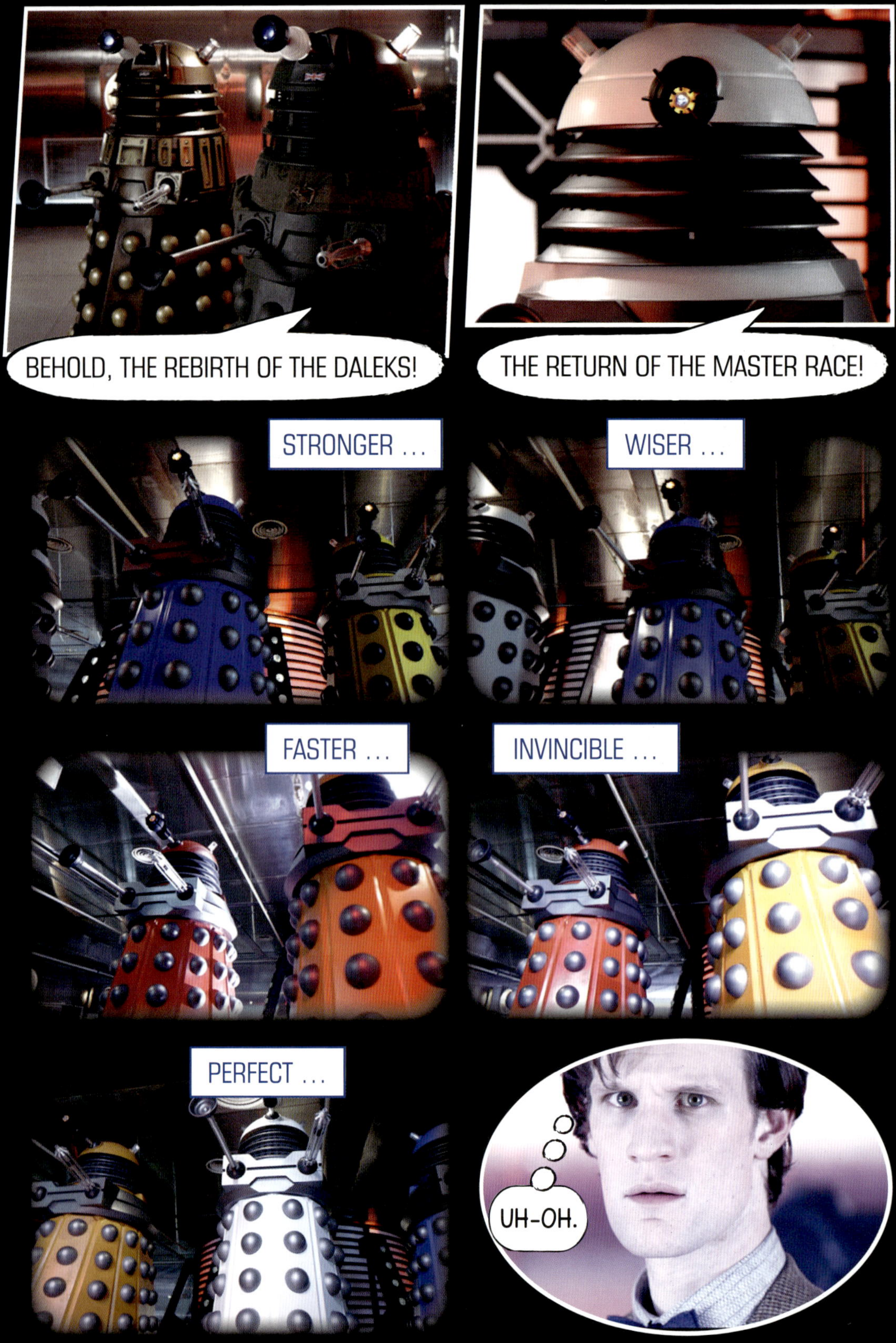
BEHOLD, THE REBIRTH OF THE DALEKS!
THE RETURN OF THE MASTER RACE!
STRONGER ...
WISER ...
FASTER ...
INVINCIBLE ...
PERFECT ...
UH-OH.

BRACEWELL! THIS IS NO TIME TO BE MOPING.
THAT'S ALL YOU'VE GOT TO SAY TO HIM? I THOUGHT YOU ARE FAMOUS FOR INSPIRING PEOPLE TO ...
I HAVE NO TIME TO BE INSPIRING! BRACEWELL! BE A MAN AND –
THAT'S JUST IT – I'M *NOT* A MAN! THOSE CREATURES MADE ME.
YET I CAN REMEMBER SO MANY THINGS. THE LAST WAR – THE DEAD – THE AWFUL MISERY OF IT ALL.
YES, AND MAYBE YOU'LL WANT TO HELP US AVOID THEM THIS TIME ROUND. THERE'S A SPACESHIP UP THERE LIGHTING UP LONDON LIKE A CHRISTMAS TREE AND THOUSANDS OF PEOPLE WILL DIE. YOU'RE THE ONLY ONE WHO CAN HELP TAKE IT DOWN.
I AM?
YOU'RE ALIEN TECHNOLOGY, TOO – AS CLEVER AS THE DALEKS, SO START THINKING! WHAT ABOUT SOME KIND OF MISSILE ...?
WELL, WITH A GRAVITY BUBBLE, I SUPPOSE IT'S *POSSIBLE*
YES, BUT WE NEED TO SEND SOMETHING UP THERE **NOW**. CAN THAT BE DONE, BRACEWELL?

Meanwhile, the beam from the Dalek ship continues to fire on London. Steadily. Effectively.
Ruthlessly.
Elsewhere on their ship, the Daleks demonstrate a different kind of ruthlessness.
ALL HAIL THE NEW DALEKS! ALL HAIL THE NEW DALEKS!
YOU ARE INFERIOR!
YES!
YES!
THEN PREPARE!
WE ARE READY!
CLEANSE THE UNCLEAN! WIPE THEM OUT!

DISINTEGRATE!
ffiiiiiii zzzzzzzZZH!!!
ffiiiiiii zzzzzzzZZ- ka-PROW!!!
BLIMEY, WHAT DO YOU DO TO THE ONES WHO ACTUALLY MESS UP?
YOU ARE THE DOCTOR! YOU MUST BE EXTERMINATED!
DON'T MESS WITH ME, SWEETHEART!
BRAVE TALK. BUT I'M NOT THE ONE THEY'RE MESSING WITH – IT'S AMY AND EVERYONE ELSE IN LONDON WHO'S REALLY IN DANGER.

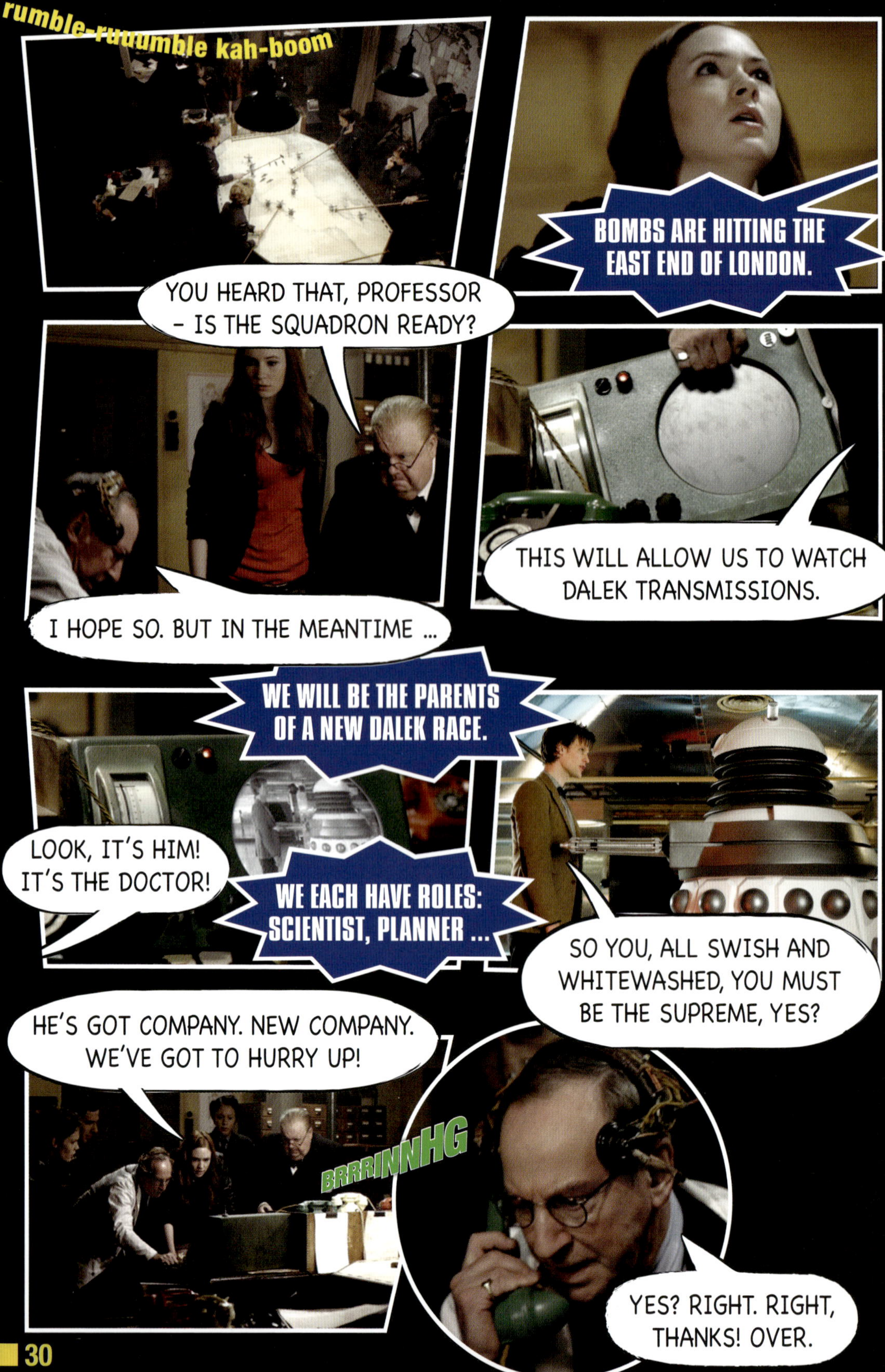
rumble-ruuumble kah-boom
BOMBS ARE HITTING THE EAST END OF LONDON.
YOU HEARD THAT, PROFESSOR - IS THE SQUADRON READY?
I HOPE SO. BUT IN THE MEANTIME ...
THIS WILL ALLOW US TO WATCH DALEK TRANSMISSIONS.
WE WILL BE THE PARENTS OF A NEW DALEK RACE.
LOOK, IT'S HIM! IT'S THE DOCTOR!
WE EACH HAVE ROLES: SCIENTIST, PLANNER ...
SO YOU, ALL SWISH AND WHITEWASHED, YOU MUST BE THE SUPREME, YES?
HE'S GOT COMPANY. NEW COMPANY. WE'VE GOT TO HURRY UP!
BRRRINNHG
YES? RIGHT. RIGHT, THANKS! OVER.

PRIME MINISTER, WE NOW HAVE THE EXACT LOCATION OF THE DALEK SPACESHIP.
SPLENDID! GO TO IT, GROUP CAPTAIN!
YES, SIR! BROADSWORD TO DANNY BOY! SCRAMBLE! SCRAMBLE!
QUESTION IS, WHAT DO WE DO NOW? EITHER YOU TURN OFF YOUR CLEVER MACHINE OR I BLOW YOU AND YOUR NEW MASTER RACE INTO ETERNITY.
AND YOU WITH US.
THAT COMES WITH THE JOB, I'M AFRAID.
MY SCAN REVEALS TARDIS SELF-DESTRUCT DEVICE IS NON-EXISTENT!
ALL RIGHT, I CONFESS – IT'S A JAM BISCUIT.
BUT I *WAS* PROMISED TEA, YOU'LL RECALL!
But before the Daleks can punish the Doctor for tricking him –
RRRRRRRRRROOOOO!
RRRRRRRRRROOOOO!
RRRRRRRRRROOOOO!
ALERT! UNIDENTIFIED PROJECTILES ARE APPROACHING!
WHAT HAVE THE HUMANS DONE, DOCTOR?
EXPLAIN!
EXPLAIN!!
EXPLAIN!!!

DANNY BOY TO THE DOCTOR! DANNY BOY TO THE DOCTOR! ARE YOU RECEIVING ME? OVER.
YES, I'M RECEIVING –
The Doctor can't see what's happening, but he can imagine it well enough: 20th century aeroplanes taking on an enemy from beyond the stars!
OH, WINSTON! YOU BEAUTY!
DANNY BOY TO THE DOCTOR! COME IN. OVER.
LOUD AND CLEAR, DANNY BOY! BIG DISH ON SIDE OF ALIEN SHIP – BLOW IT UP! OVER!
It is this last command in particular that the Daleks do not take kindly to.
EXTERMINATE THE DOCTOR!
EXTERMINATE!!

YOU LOVE THOSE 'EX-' WORDS, DON'T YOU? IN THAT CASE, HOPE YOU DON'T MIND IF I "EXIT"!
YOU HEARD THE DOCTOR, DANNY BOY. TARGET THE DISH AND STOP THAT BEAM! OVER.
UNDERSTOOD, GROUP CAPTAIN. OVER.
OKAY CHAPS, LET'S PUT LONDON BACK UNDER COVER OF DARKNESS!
TALLY HO!
COVER ME – I'M GOING IN CLOSE!

PULL OUT, PULL OUT!
NO!
WE'VE LOST A PLANE, SIR! OVER.
THE BEAM IS STILL WORKING, SIR.
THEN SEND THEM IN AGAIN!
The RAF planes regroup and attack again.
But the Daleks' superior technology seems to be gaining the upper hand.
DANNY BOY TO THE DOCTOR ...
ONLY ME LEFT NOW, AND THE DISH SEEMS TO BE PROTECTED. ANYTHING YOU CAN DO, SIR? OVER.

THE DOCTOR TO DANNY BOY. I CAN DISRUPT THE DALEK SHIELDS, BUT NOT FOR LONG. OVER.
GOOD SHOW, DOCTOR, GO TO IT! OVER.
So 'Danny Boy' makes one more heroic approach.
While in the TARDIS ...
HE'S ALREADY GOING IN –
THAT MEANS HE'S COUNTING ON ME – IF I CAN'T TAKE OUT THE SHIELDS, THEN HE'S A **SITTING DUCK** ...!
WHAT IS HAPPENING?
THE SHIELDS ARE DOWN!
And with the Daleks' shields down ...
There is no sound in space. But if there were, this moment would sound something like this ...
SCREAAAAZZZAKKKK!
NO! THE ENERGY PULSE IS DESTROYED!

OH, THANK GOODNESS FOR THE DARKNESS OF NIGHT!
DIRECT HIT, SIR!
THE LIGHTS! THE LIGHTS ARE OFF AGAI
DOCTOR!! CALL OFF THAT FINAL PLANE! CALL OFF YOUR ATTACK!
NO, NOT THIS TIME. THIS IS THE END FOR YOU! AS SOON AS DANNY BOY ATTACKS YOU'LL BE GONE FOR GOOD!
CALL OFF THE ATTACK OR WE WILL DESTROY THE EARTH.
I'M NOT STUPID, MATE! YOU'VE JUST PLAYED YOUR LAST CARD!
NO, *THIS* IS THE LAST 'CARD', AS YOU CALL IT:
BRACEWELL ... IS A BOMB.

YOU'RE BLUFFING. LYING'S SECOND NATURE TO YOU.
AT BRACEWELL'S CORE IS A SOURCE OF UNTOLD POWER. CALL OFF YOUR ATTACK OR WE WILL BLOW HIM UP.
NO! THIS IS MY BEST CHANCE EVER! I CAN RID THE UNIVERSE OF YOU DALEKS, ONCE AND FOR ALL!
THEN DO IT. BUT THE EARTH WILL DIE SCREAMING!
AND IF I LET YOU GO, YOU'LL BE STRONGER THAN EVER. A NEW RACE OF DALEKS.
THEN CHOOSE, DOCTOR! DESTROY THE DALEKS OR SAVE THE EARTH. WE WILL NOW BEGIN THE COUNTDOWN!
CHOOSE, DOCTOR!
CHOOSE!!

THE DOCTOR TO DANNY BOY. THE DOCTOR TO DANNY BOY ... WITHDRAW.
BUT SIR ...!
WITHDRAW AND RETURN TO EARTH. WITH ANY LUCK I'LL SEE YOU THERE. OVER AND OUT.
POLICE BOX
COME ON, YOU BLASTED OLD-MODEL TARDIS. CAN'T YOU MATERIALISE FASTER THAN THIS?
Only seconds later the Doctor dashes into the map room and ...
POW!
DOCTOR!
SO SORRY ABOUT THAT, PROFESSOR, BUT YOU'RE A BOMB! AN INDESCRIBABLY MASSIVE DALEK BOMB!
WHAT???
AND TO ADD INSULT TO INJURY, I'M GOING TO HAVE TO REQUEST THAT YOU PLEASE REMOVE YOUR SHIRT ...

And so ...
I DON'T KNOW WHAT TO DO. I'VE NEVER SEEN ONE OF THESE UP CLOSE BEFORE!
SO, THEY'VE WIRED HIM UP?
NO, NOT WIRED HIM UP! HE *IS* A BOMB. WALKING, TALKING AND ... WELL, YOU GET THE IDEA.
YES, AND THE MOMENT THAT ENTIRE DIAL FLASHES RED, WE'LL *ALL* BE GETTING THE IDEA!
BUT I DON'T UNDERSTAND – HE TALKED TO US ABOUT HIS MEMORIES. THE GREAT WAR ...
THOSE WERE FAKE MEMORIES IMPLANTED INTO HIS COMPUTERISED BRAIN. BUT THAT GIVES ME AN IDEA ...
TALK TO ME, BRACEWELL. TELL ME ABOUT YOUR LIFE!

DOCTOR, I REALLY DON'T THINK THIS IS THE TIME!
BUT HOW CAN I –
I'M NOT TRYING TO GET TO KNOW YOU BETTER IN OUR FINAL MOMENTS TOGETHER! I NEED YOU TO TELL ME BECAUSE YOU NEED TO PROVE YOU'RE HUMAN!
THAT IS, HOW CAN *I* PROVE TO YOU ...?
NOT TO US, PROFESSOR.
THANK YOU, AMY.
TO *YOURSELF*. YOU'RE THE ONE WHO NEEDS CONVINCING.
LISTEN, WE HAVE PRECIOUS LITTLE TIME. EVEN AS WE SPEAK THE DALEKS ARE GLOATING AS THEY PREPARE TO LEAVE OUR LITTLE SECTION OF THE UNIVERSE.
COUNTDOWN PROCEEDING!

Bracewell tries to remember ...
WELL, MY FAMILY RAN THE POST OFFICE. IT WAS A LITTLE PLACE JUST NEAR THE ABBEY. JUST BY THE ASH TREES.
VERY GOOD, DETAILS ARE HELPFUL. WHAT ABOUT *EMOTIONAL* MEMORIES?
YOUR PARENTS! FOCUS ON THEM ...
GOOD PEOPLE. KIND PEOPLE. THEY ...
THEY DIED. SCARLET FEVER.
WHAT WAS THAT LIKE? HOW DID IT FEEL?
PLEASE ...
EDWIN, HOW DID IT MAKE YOU FEEL? TELL ME NOW!
PLEASE, IT **HURTS**. AND SO BADLY, DOCTOR. LIKE A WOUND.
ACTUALLY ... IT WAS WORSE THAN A
THERE WAS

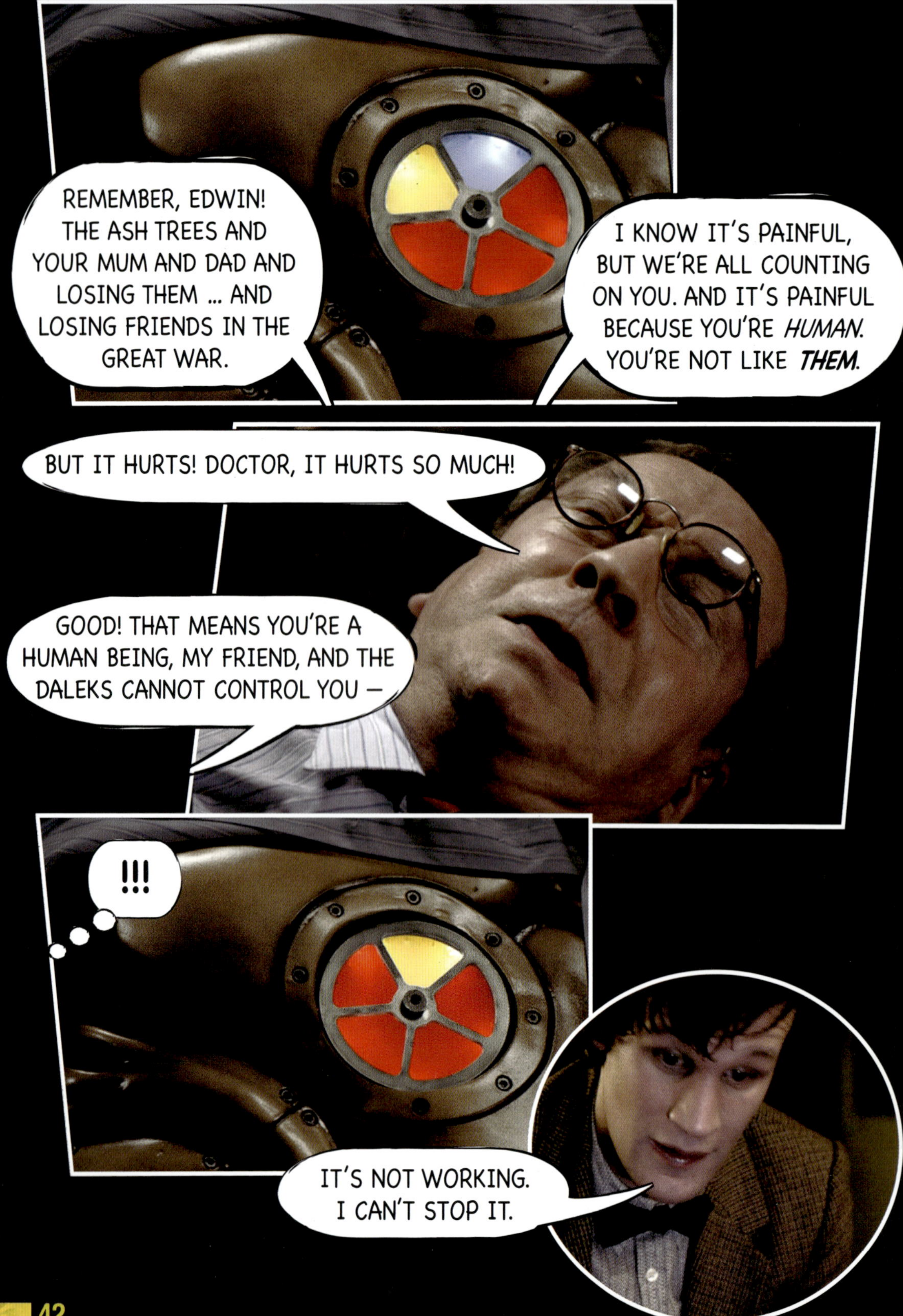
REMEMBER, EDWIN! THE ASH TREES AND YOUR MUM AND DAD AND LOSING THEM ... AND LOSING FRIENDS IN THE GREAT WAR.
I KNOW IT'S PAINFUL, BUT WE'RE ALL COUNTING ON YOU. AND IT'S PAINFUL BECAUSE YOU'RE *HUMAN*. YOU'RE NOT LIKE ***THEM***.
BUT IT HURTS! DOCTOR, IT HURTS SO MUCH!
GOOD! THAT MEANS YOU'RE A HUMAN BEING, MY FRIEND, AND THE DALEKS CANNOT CONTROL YOU –
!!!
IT'S NOT WORKING. I CAN'T STOP IT.

DOCTOR, LET'S TRY SOME OTHER EMOTIONS.
EDWIN, WAS THERE SOMEONE YOU CARED ABOUT - SOMEONE YOU PERHAPS HAVEN'T SEEN IN A LONG TIME ...?
YES. YES, THERE WAS.
DORABELLA.
DORABELLA? THAT'S A LOVELY NAME, A *BEAUTIFUL* NAME. WHAT WAS SHE LIKE?
OH, SUCH A SMILE. AND HER EYES WERE SO BLUE THEY WERE ALMOST VIOLET. LIKE THE LAST TOUCH OF SUNSET ON THE EDGE OF THE WORLD.
DORABELLA.
YAY!! Hooray
WELCOME TO THE HUMAN RACE, BRACEWELL! ACTUALLY, WELCOME BACK ALL OF US TO THE LAND OF THE LIVING ...!
THE BRACEWELL BOMB IS INACTIVE.
IMPOSSIBLE!
PREPARE FOR TIME-JUMP IN ONE MINUTE!

The Earth now safe once again, the Doctor rushes off to pursue the Daleks before it's too late.

Epilogue

An hour passes, but the Doctor and Amy have yet to board the TARDIS for departure.

Both feel the need to make sure that someone they have grown to care about does not become one of history's loose ends ...

EDWIN – I THOUGHT I DISTINCTLY HEARD THE PM TELL YOU NOT TO MOPE.

AH, THERE'S NO USE TRYING TO SOFTEN THE BLOW, MISS POND.
THE BLOW?
YES, I KNOW WHY YOU'RE HERE.

YES, IT'S BECAUSE WE WANTED TO MAKE SURE –

– THAT I WAS DEACTIVATED, I KNOW.
YOU SEE, I'VE BEEN EXPECTING BOTH OF YOU. I KNEW THIS MOMENT HAD TO COME.

AH, I SEE ...
UM, YES. SO DO I.
I SUPPOSE THERE'S NO CHANCE OF EVER FOOLING YOU, IS THERE, PROFESSOR?
I DON'T HOLD IT AGAINST YOU. YOU HAVE NO CHOICE. I'M DALEK TECHNOLOGY. CAN'T ALLOW ME TO GO POTTERING AROUND DOWN HERE.
The Doctor and Amy exchange glances ... and in those glances, a **plan** is born.
NO, YOU'RE DEAD RIGHT, PROFESSOR. AND BY THE TIME I GET BACK HERE IN ... WHAT, FIFTEEN MINUTES?
MORE LIKE TWENTY.
TWENTY MINUTES, YEAH. YOU ARE GOING TO BE SO DE-ACTIVATED. IT'S GOING BE LIKE YOU'VE NEVER EVEN BEEN ... ACTIVATED.
VERY WELL, DOCTOR. I SHALL WAIT HERE AND PREPARE MYSELF FOR ...
ACTUALLY, ANY POSSIBILITY THAT IT COULD TAKE HALF AN HOUR?

EASILY! YES, THAT'S MUCH MORE REALISTIC. SO NO PACKING UP AND RUNNING OFF DURING THAT HALF HOUR, WILL YOU? DON'T GO TRYING TO FIND THOSE ASH TREES OR ...
WHAT WAS HER NAME?
YOU MEAN DORABELLA.
Soon after ...
OH, THANK YOU!
THANK YOU, BOTH OF YOU, FOR ALL YOU'VE DONE ...!
I WISH I COULD CURE MY BLUES AS EASILY AS BRACEWELL JUST DID HIS.
YES, I KNOW HOW DISAPPOINTING IT MUST BE TO HAVE THE DALEKS SLIP AWAY LIKE THAT.
BUT REMEMBER, IT HASN'T *ALL* BEEN NEGATIVE, HAS IT?

GOOD POINT. THIS HAS BEEN MORE OF A VICTORY THAN A DEFEAT, HASN'T IT?
OF COURSE. THE DALEKS LIVED TO FIGHT ANOTHER DAY, BUT SO DID YOU.
YOU'RE STARTING TO SOUND LIKE MY FRIEND WINSTON – YOU KNOW THE ENEMY WILL ALWAYS BE THERE, AND ONE'S JOB IS JUST TO KEEP SOLDIERING ON AND NOT GET DISCOURAGED.
WHICH I SUPPOSE MEANS THAT THE DALEKS WILL ALWAYS BE AROUND, AND I'LL ALWAYS BE THERE TO FIGHT THEM.
I AGREE WITH EVERYTHING EXCEPT THE LAST PART. ABOUT THAT, YOU'RE JUST DEAD WRONG.
I AM? HOW?
WE WILL ALWAYS BE THERE TO FIGHT THEM.
HMMM, YOU KNOW SOMETHING, MISS POND? YOU'RE NOT TOO SHABBY YOURSELF ...